Magic Case

The Use of Poetry in the Expanding of Consciousness

SPECIAL COMMEMORATIVE EDITION

George Trevelyan

Gateway Books, Bath, UK

*First published in 1980 by
Coventure Ltd, London*

This Edition published 1996 by

GATEWAY BOOKS
*The Hollies, Wellow,
Bath, BA2 8QJ*

*Copyright © 1980 by George Trevelyan
1996 by the Estate of George Trevelyan*

*No part of this book may be reproduced
in any form without permission from
the Publisher, except for the
quotation of brief passages
in criticism.*

*Cover design by The Design House, Bristol
Cover photos: Nicholas Toyne
Printed and bound by Redwood Books of Trowbridge*

*British Cataloguing-in Publication Data:
A catalogue record for this book is
available from the British Library*

ISBN 1-85860-047-2

The Poems

Ralph Waldo Trine	'Let there be many windows'	2
Anna Kingsford	'The Poet'	3
William Blake	from 'Jerusalem'	5
William Blake	'Fourfold Vision'	6
William Wordsworth	Sonnet: 'The World'	6
William Wordsworth	Opening verses of 'Ode: Intimations of Immortality'	7
William Wordsworth	Lines from 'Tintern Abbey'	8
Francis Thompson	From 'Mistress of Vision'	8
Francis Thompson	'In no strange land'	10
Charles Earle	'Bodily Extension'	11
Martin Armstrong	'The Cage'	12
Edmund Spenser	'The Soul'	13
S.T. Coleridge	From 'Religious Musings'	13
Thomas Traherne	'You will never enjoy the world'	15
Thomas Traherne	From 'My Spirit'	15
Thomas Traherne	From 'The Preparative'	17
William Wordsworth	From 'Ode: Intimations of Immortality'	18
Johann Wolfgang Goethe	From 'Seelige Sehnsucht'	19
W.B. Yeats	From 'Sailing to Byzantium'	19

i

T.S. Eliot	Lines from 'East Coker'	20
Edmund Waller	Last verses	20
Bhagavad Gita		21
Sidney Royse Lysaght	'We have dreamed dreams'	21
Anon	'It is eight weeks beloved'	22
Raymond Rossiter	'Christus Consolator'	23
John Donne	'Since I am coming to that Holy Roome'	25
Rabindranath Tagore (translation of Kabir)	'O Friend, hope for Him'	25
Edward FitzGerald	'Rubaiyat of Omar Khayyam'. Five verses	26
Francis Thompson	From 'The Hound of Heaven'	28
Robert Frost	'Trial by Existence'	29
Swami Vivekanander	'The Cup'	32
William Shakespeare	From 'Measure for Measure'	32
Robert Browning	From 'Paracelsus'	33
John Masefield	'Here in the self'	33
Karle Wilson Baker	'My life is a tree'	34
Juan Ramon Jiminez	'I have the feeling'	34
T.E. Brown	'Indwelling'	35
Edward Carpenter	'There is no peace'	35
David Gascoyne	'Not in my lifetime'	37
Frederick Myers	'A Cosmic Outlook'	38
Sidney Carter	'Your holy hearsay'	38
Joseph Plunkett	'I see His blood'	39
Gerard Manley Hopkins	'Hurrahing in Harvest'	40
Gerard Manley Hopkins	'As Kingfishers catch fire'	41
Bhagavad Gita	Krishna's Return	42
Djwhal Khul	'The Great Invocation'	42

Edwin Muir	'Transfiguration'	43
Gerard Manley Hopkins	'God's Grandeur'	44
D.H. Lawrence	'The Song of a Man who has Come Through'	45
Thalia Gage	From 'Prelude to Pentecost'	46
Stephen Spender	'I think continually'	46
Evelyn Nolt	'The Glory which is Earth'	47
George Griffiths	'Nexus'	48
Christopher Fry	From 'A Sleep of Prisoners'	49
James Elroy Flecker	'Awake, awake'	50
F.C. Happold	'A wind has blown ...'	50
Walter de la Mare	'Song of the Shadows'	53

Acknowledgements

For permission to use copyright material, the author gratefully makes the following acknowledgements.

To Clarendon Press Ltd, Oxford, for *Bodily Extension* by J.C. Earle and for lines from *A Sleep of Prisoners* by Christopher Fry: to MacMillan & Co., Ltd, for verses from *Sailing to Byzantium* by W.B. Yeats: to Faber & Faber, Ltd, for lines from *East Coker* by T.S. Eliot, and 'I think continually...' by Stephen Spender, and from *Transfiguration* by Edwin Muir: to Allen & Unwin, Ltd, for lines from *Towards Democracy* by Edward Carpenter: to Oxford University Press for *Not in My Lifetime*... by David Gascogne: to Mrs George Griffiths, for the poem *Nexus* by her husband: to the Masefield Trustees (The Society of Authors) for a sonnet by Masefield: to Jonathan Cape, Ltd, and the Estate of Robert Frost for *Trial by Existence* by Robert Frost: to Laurence Pollinger, Ltd, and the Estate of the late Mrs. Frieda Lawrence Ravagli, for D.H. Lawrence's '*The Song of a Man who has come through*'.

Magic Casements

The Use of Poetry in the Expanding of Consciousness

This little anthology has a special purpose. We are concerned with the use of poetry as an instrument for widening of consciousness. For many people, poetry has somewhat dropped out of life. In our over-masculinated society, in which logical analysing intellect is used to gain our ends, the more feminine intuitive faculties are often allowed to go dormant. But these are precisely the faculties that make poetry. True imagination can blend with the being within form, and rediscover the miraculous oneness of all life. The poet is one who can crystallize into words this profound experience of identity. Thus, if we can take those words and work our imagination livingly into them, we may ourselves experience the 'vision of wholeness' in our souls. So poetry rightly used and rethought can become an instrument for awakening the atrophied organs of perception of the invisible words, the '... magic casements opening on the foam of perilous seas and faery lands forlorn'.

This collection is made up of poems which I have often quoted in lectures on the spiritual awakening of our time, given at Attingham and on Wrekin Trust conferences. I am frequently asked by students for copies of these poems. Well, here they are. This is not an academic study, but a personal choice of poems used to illustrate in better words than mine the reality of the inner worlds of being. In our time there is an awakening to an 'holistic' vision of life. This involves a quickening of the spirit, a throwing wide of consciousness to encompass the eternal oneness of life, reaching beyond the restriction and limitation of sense-bound thinking.

To achieve this we must allow the imaginative and intuitive side of our nature to flower, and be prepared to step beyond the limitations of old thinking patterns. Thus, let us start with a quotation from *RALPH WALDO TRINE*'s classic 'In Tune with the Infinite'.

> Let there be many windows in your soul
> That all the glory of the universe
> May beautify it. Not the narrow pane
> Of one poor creed can catch the radiant rays
> That shine from countless sources. Tear away
> The blinds of superstition; let the light
> Pour through fair windows broad as truth itself
> And high as Heaven.
> Why should the spirit peer
> Through some priest-curtained orifice, and grope
> Along dim corridors of doubt, when all
> The splendour from unfathomed seas of space
> Might bathe it with their golden seas of love?
> Sweep up the debris of decaying faiths,
> Sweep down the cobwebs of worn-out beliefs,
> And throw your soul wide open to the light
> Of reason and of knowledge. Tune your ear
> To all the wordless music of the stars,
> And to the voice of nature, and your heart
> Shall turn to truth and goodness, as the plant

Turns to the sun. A thousand unseen hands
Reach down to help you from their peace-
crowned heights,
And all the forces of the firmament
Shall fortify your strength. Be not afraid
To thrust aside half-truths and grasp the whole.

And now, to grasp what the poetic faculty means, let us take *ANNA KINGSFORD*'s words:

The poet hath no self apart from his larger Self. His personality is Divine; and being Divine it hath no limits.

He is supreme and ubiquitous in consciousness; his heart beats in every element.

The pulses of the Infinite Deep of Heaven vibrate in his own; and responding to their strength and their plenitude, he feels more intensely than other men.

Not merely he sees and examines these Rocks and Trees; these variable waters and these glittering peaks.

Not merely he hears this plaintive wind, these rolling peals.

But he is all these, and when he sings, it is not he — the Man — whose voice is heard; it is the voice of all Manifold Nature herself.

In his voice the Sunshine laughs; the Mountains give forth their sonorous Echoes; the swift lightnings flash.

The great continual Cadence of Universal Life moves and becomes articulate in human language.

So we are really concerned with the faculty of uniting with the being within form, which of course is wholly invisible to the normal looking with physical sight. This sense-bound thinking alone can never penetrate to the living essence of things. This is the task of the Imagination, which in *COLERIDGE*'s phrase is:

> The repetition in the finite mind of the eternal act of Creation in the infinite I AM.

Keats wrote: I am certain of nothing but the holiness of the heart's affection and the truth of imagination.

And Shelley: Poetry is the breath and finer spirit of all knowledge; it is the impassioned expression on the face of science.

And Einstein: Science without religion is blind and religion without science is lame.

And Rudolf Steiner: We are forced on to recognise the existence of objects over and above those we experience in sense perception. Such objects are Ideas. In taking possession of the Idea, thinking merges itself into the World Mind. What was working without now works within. Man has become one with the World Being at its highest potency. Such a becoming-realized of the Idea is the true communion of man.

WILLIAM BLAKE, that great prophet of the New Age, speaks of his purpose as teacher, artist and poet:

> ... I rest not from my great task!
> To open the Eternal Worlds, to open the
>   immortal Eyes
> Of Man inwards into the Worlds of Thought,
>   into Eternity
> Ever expanding in the Bosom of God, the
>   Human Imagination.
> O Saviour, pour upon me thy Spirit of meekness
>   and love!
> Annihilate the Selfhood in me; be thou all
>   my life!

And, as Blake states in prose:

> This world of Imagination is the world of Eternity. It is the bosom into which we shall go after death of the vegetated body. This world of Imagination is Infinite and Eternal, whereas the world of generation and vegetation is finite and temporal. All things are comprehended in their Eternal Forms in the divine body of the Saviour, the true voice of Eternity, the Human Imagination.

Blake knew very well that the acute development of intellectual knowledge was achieved at the price of losing perception of the spiritual worlds. It meant a narrowing of vision so that we stand over against things to analyse them as mere observer. No longer can we unite with the 'being' within them. To him this 'onlooker consciousness' was a kind of sleep condition, as opposed to his own 'fourfold vision', which sees every living thing as it is in its eternal reality.

Thus he writes:

> Now I with a fourfold vision see
> And a fourfold vision is given to me
> Fourfold in my supreme delight
> And threefold in soft Beulah's night
> And two-fold always. May God us keep
> From single vision, and Newton's sleep.

WORDSWORTH shared this sense of the tragic loss through intellectual investigation which loses touch with the intuitive imagination.

> Sweet is the lore that nature brings.
> Our meddling intellect
> Destroys the beauteous form of things
> We murder to dissect.

The Life of the Whole cannot be explored without the developing of subtler faculties of perception and an intensifying of imaginative thinking. Wordsworth reflects the longing of the soul — its nostalgia for the realm from which it is increasingly divorced through intellectual materialism. This is expressed in a great sonnet.

> The world is too much with us; late and soon,
> Getting and spending, we lay waste our powers;
> Little we see in nature that is ours,
> We have given our hearts away, a sordid boon!
> This sea that bares her bosom to the moon;

The winds that will be howling at all hours,
And are up-gathered now like sleeping flowers;
For this, for everything, we are out of tune,
It moves not. — Great God! I'd rather be
A pagan suckled in a creed outworn,
So might I, standing on this pleasant lea,
Have glimpses that would make me less forlorn;
Have sight of Proteus rising from the sea,
Or hear old Triton blow his wreathéd horn.

Wordsworth had the gift of inner vision into the 'etheric' world which vitalizes and animates the whole of nature, and for many of us, in our youth, the faculties for perception of this realm are still active.

> There was a time when meadow, grove, and stream,
>   The earth, and every common sight,
>   To me did seem
>   Apparelled in celestial light,
> The glory and the freshness of a dream.
> It is not now as it hath been of yore; —
>   Turn wheresoe'er I may,
>   By night or day,
> The things which I have seen I now can see no more.
>
>   The Rainbow comes and goes,
>   And lovely is the Rose,
>   The Moon doth with delight
> Look round her when the heavens are bare,
>   Waters on a starry night
>   Are beautiful and fair;
> The sunshine is a glorious birth;
> But yet I know, where'er I go,

That there hath past away a glory from the earth...
...Whither is fled the visionary gleam?
Where is it now, the glory and the dream?

In the famous lines composed at Tintern Abbey, the youthful glory is replaced by a deeper experience:

>...And I have felt
A presence that disturbs me with the joy
Of elevated thoughts; a sense sublime
Of something far more deeply interfused,
Whose dwelling is the light of setting suns,
And the round ocean and the living air,
And the blue sky, and in the mind of man:
A motion and a spirit, that impels
All thinking things, all objects of all thought,
And rolls through all things.

Indeed, we belong to these eternal worlds, and to find our way back to them is the goal of the soul's awakening. After the experience of separation by the drastic limitation of incarnation in a physical body, we can enmember ourselves again with the great Oneness. This longing and this hope are expressed by *FRANCIS THOMPSON* in 'The Mistress of Vision', of which I quote only a few lines. The soul speaks and the answer comes from the higher self:

> Where is the land of Luthany,
> Where is the tract of Elenore?
> I am bound therefor.
> 'Pierce thy heart to find the key;
> With thee take

Only what none else would keep:
Learn to dream when thou dost wake,
Learn to wake when thou dost sleep...
When thy seeing blindeth thee
To what thy fellow mortals see
When their sight to thee is sightless;
Their living death; their light, most lightless;
Search no more —
Pass the gates of Luthany, tread the region Elenore.'
Where is the land of Luthany,
And where the region Elenore?
I do faint therefor.
'When to the new eyes of thee
All things by immortal power
Near or far,
Hiddenly
To each other linkéd are,
That thou canst not stir a flower
Without troubling of a star;
... Seek no more!
Pass the gates of Luthany, tread the region Elenore.'

It is, of course, easy to say this feelingly, but the thought must not be allowed to masquerade as the real experience — which for most of us can only be a remote goal. But the goal and the way are closely united, and the first essential is to grasp the concept of a wholeness of which we are an integral part.

FRANCIS THOMPSON's great and well-known poem 'In No Strange Land' shows how close to us is this other world:

O world invisible, we view thee,
O world intangible, we touch thee,
O world unknowable, we know thee,
Inapprehensible, we clutch thee!

Does the fish soar to find the ocean,
The eagle plunge to find the air —
That we ask the stars in motion
If they have rumour of thee there?

Not where the wheeling systems darken,
And our benumbed conceiving soars!
The drift of pinions, would we hearken,
Beats at our own clay-shuttered doors.

The angels keep their ancient places;
Turn but a stone and start a wing!
'Tis ye, 'tis your estranged faces,
That miss the many-splendoured thing.

But (when so sad thou canst not sadder)
Cry; — and upon thy so sore loss
Shall shine the traffic of Jacob's ladder
Pitched betwixt Heaven and Charing Cross.

Yea, in the night, my Soul, my daughter,
Cry, — clinging Heaven by the hems;
And lo, Christ walking on the water
Not of Gennesareth, but Thames!

It is indeed a great marvel and paradox that, by entering inwards, we can move through and so discover that our consciousness can indeed expand to encompass the breadth of the universe. As Andrew Glazewski used to say:

> Your consciousness is not in your body:
> your body is in your consciousness.

CHARLES JAMES EARLE expresses this important principle in his sonnet 'Bodily Extension':

> The body is not bounded by its skin:
>   Its effluence, like a gentle cloud of scent,
>   Is wide into the air diffused, and blent
> With elements unseen, its way doth win,
> To ether frontiers where take origin
>   Far subtler systems, nobler regions meant
>   To be the area and the instrument
> Of operations ever to begin
> Anew and never end. Thus every man
>   Wears as his robe the garment of the sky —
> So close his union with the cosmic plan,
>   So perfectly he pierces low and high,
> Reaching as far in space as creature can
>   And co-extending with immensity.

Note the 'ether frontiers' which we must cross. Our rockets are fired for the exploration of physical space, but there is another form of space exploration in the expansion of consciousness. To this, there can be no end. We are beginning to explore the frequency bands and up into subtler systems, reaching like Dante towards the Empyrean. Modern spiritual research has familiarized us with that field of unified vital energies and forces which plays with infinite diversity into every form, and holds together the particles comprising visible objects in all the kingdoms of nature. But cold intellect alone cannot attain the experience of this all-pervading unity. It can study the form, but the being within the form remains inaccessible to it.

We must awaken in ourselves the dormant faculties of higher perception. This involves the development of subtler senses. If we are to begin to experience the realm of higher realities, we must discover and employ the inner eye, the inner power of listening, a subtler sense of thought. For the five accepted senses are really filters to protect man from the power of the universe. The soul in incarnation takes upon itself the protective sheaths of the physical, etheric and astral bodies in order to function effectively in the density of earth's gravity-field. We might compare it to a diver donning a heavy diving-suit in order to explore the wonders at the bottom of the sea. Another metaphor is provided by *MARTIN ARMSTRONG* in 'The Cage':

> Man, afraid to be alive
> Shuts his soul in senses five,
> From fields of uncreated light
> Into the crystal tower of sight,
> And from the roaring songs of space
> Into the small flesh-carven place
> Of the ear whose cave impounds
> Only small and broken sounds,
> And to his narrow sense of touch
> From strength that held the stars in clutch,
> And from the warm ambrosial spice
> Of flowers and fruits of paradise,
> Into the frail and fitful power
> Of scent and tasting, sweet and sour;
> And toiling for a sordid wage
> There in his self-created cage

> Ah, how safely barred is he
> From menace of Eternity.

Birth is indeed to be seen as a descent of a free-ranging spiritual being into the severe limitations of a body; and we shall learn to see death as truly a rebirth and release into a plane of light. To appreciate this, we must overcome the natural identification with our lower self and awaken to the great truth that we possess a self that is higher — a spiritual member of our greater being. This appreciation is the gateway to an experience of ourselves as participating in the whole. It is the true 're-membering'. For the New Age vision is re-establishing man as a being of spirit, soul and body; and we may be certain that a droplet of divinity cannot be extinguished by the discarding of the worn-out body. Here is a verse from *EDMUND SPENSER*:

> So every spirit as it is more pure,
> And hath in it the more of heavenly light,
> So it the fairer body doth procure
> To habit in, and it more fairly dight
> With cheerful grace and amiable sight,
> For of the soul the body form doth take,
> And soul is form and doth the body make.

In the same connection, it is worth considering this quotation from *COLERIDGE*'s 'Religious Musings':

> There is one Mind, one omnipresent Mind
> Omnific. His most holy name is Love.
> Truth of subliming import...
>   'Tis the sublime in man,

Our noontide Majesty, to know ourselves
Parts and proportions of one wondrous whole.
This fraternises man. ...

  Toy-bewitched,
Made blind by lusts, disinherited of soul,
No common centre Man, no common sire
Knoweth! A sordid solitary thing
Mid countless brethren with a lonely heart
Through courts and cities the smooth savage roams,
Feeling himself, his own low self, the whole;
When he by sacred sympathy might make
The Whole one Self! Self that no alien knows,
Self, far diffused as fancy's wing can travel!
Self, spreading still! Oblivious of its own
Yet all of all possessing! This is Faith!
This the Messiah's destined victory!

What a picture of modern man! Indeed, in our heathen culture we can be 'smooth savages'. But 'sacred sympathy', the ability to widen and intensify imaginative thinking, leads to the discovery of the divinity within all created things and our affinity with the being within all form. Thus we are led out of loneliness — a necessary phase in the development of self-awareness — to the discovery of our higher self which is the gateway to wholeness. Herein lies the triumphant challenge of the last line. It is the destined victory of the Christ, that we should each widen consciousness to find that our inner being is truly united with all life. Then we shall be able to say with *TRAHERNE*:

You will never enjoy the world aright till the sea itself floweth in your veins, till you are clothed with heavens and crowned with the stars; and perceive yourself to be the sole heir of the whole world, and more than so, because men are in it who are every one the sole heir as well as you ...

The works of the metaphysical poet *THOMAS TRAHERNE*, who died in 1674, were lost and not rediscovered until the first decade of this century. In a sense that is appropriate, for only now can his vision be truly understood. Traherne possessed the capacity to remember back into the womb and beyond, and most of his writing strives to impart the living experience of oneness with the divinity in all created things. The great discovery we are now making is that the void, or centre, we enter in meditation is indeed the magic portal through which we can pass into the eternal worlds. This is expressed by the poem, 'My Spirit', in which *TRAHERNE* struggles with the great paradox of the inner centre which is, at the same time, infinite. I quote from the closing stanzas:

> My essence was capacity
>   That felt all things ...
> That made me present evermore
>   With whatsoe'er I saw.
> An object, if it were before
> My eye, was by Dame Nature's law
>   Within my soul.
> O joy! O wonder and delight!
>   O sacred mystery!
> My soul a spirit infinite

An image of the Deity,
A pure substantial light,
  A strange mysterious sphere,
  A deep abyss
  That sees and is
The only proper place of Heavenly Bliss.
A strange extended orb of Joy
  Proceeding from within.
Which did on every side, convey
Itself, and being nigh of kin
  To God, did every way
Dilate itself even in an instant, and
Like an indivisible centre stand
At once surrounding all eternity.
  'Twas not a sphere
  Yet did appear
One infinite...
'Twas not a sphere, but 'twas a might
Invisible and yet gave light.
O wondrous Self! O sphere of light,
  O sphere of joy most fair
O act, O power infinite;
  O subtile and unbounded air!
    O living orb of sight!
Thou which within me art, yet me! Thou eye,
And temple of His whole infinity!
  O what a world art Thou! A world within!
    All things appear,
    All objects are
Alive in Thee! Supersubstantial, rare,
  Above themselves, and nigh of kin
    To those pure things we find
      In His great mind

> Who made the world! Tho' now eclipsed by sin,
>   There they are useful and divine,
>   Exalted there they ought to shine.

In 'The Preparative', Traherne describes the experience of pre-existence. This principle is of the utmost importance to us today. As we have noted, the imperishable spiritual entity survives death, for an eternal spiritual being cannot be extinguished. But that we existed as a developed soul before birth is a most vital point if we are to understand the meaning of earth life. Traherne first clearly describes the embryo:

> ... Before I skill'd to prize
>   Those living stars, mine Eyes;
> Before I knew these hands were mine
> Or that my sinews did my Members join ...
>   I was within
> A House I knew not, newly cloath'd with skin.
>
> Then was my Soul my only All to me,
>   A living endless Eye
>   Scarce bounded with the sky
> Whose Power and Act and Essence was to see;
>   I was an inward sphere of Light
>   Or an interminable Orb of Sight
>   Exceeding that which makes the days,
>   A Vital Sun, that shed abroad its rays,
>   All Life, all Sense,
>   A naked, simple, pure intelligence.

What a challenge to parents, doctors and teachers! We should indeed never think of the new-born child as a tiny soul, but as a mature soul beginning the drastic descent into a tiny frame.

WORDSWORTH expresses a similar vision in his great 'Ode: Intimations of Immortality from Recollections of Early Childhood':

> Our birth is but a sleep and a forgetting:
> The Soul that rises with us, our life's Star,
>   Hath had elsewhere its setting,
>   And cometh from afar;
>   Not in entire forgetfullness,
>   And not in utter nakedness,
> But trailing clouds of glory do we come
>   From God, who is our home:
> Heaven lies about us in our infancy!
> Shades of the prison-house begin to close
>   Upon the growing boy,
> But He beholds the light, and whence it flows,
>   He sees it in his joy;
> The Youth, who daily farther from the east
>   Must travel, still is Nature's Priest,
>   And by the vision splendid
>   Is on his way attended;
> At length the Man perceives it die away,
> And fade into the light of common day.

When this process occurs, we tend too easily to assume that the earlier light was an illusion. But surely it is for each of us, in our maturing years, to revive 'the vision splendid'. The all-important principle is that there is no renewal without a dying process, no death without a sequel of becoming and resurrection. As *GOETHE* puts it in 'Seelige Sehnsucht' (The Soul's Yearning'):

Und solang Du das nicht hast
Dieses: Stirb und werde!
Bist Du nur ein trüber Gast
Auf der dunklen Erde.

(And so long as this you lack,
This dying and becoming,
You will be but a dull guest
On the darkling earth.)

WILLIAM BUTLER YEATS was similarly aware of the potentiality for renewal as the ageless soul experiences the ageing of the body. In 'Sailing to Byzantium', he writes:

> That is no country for old men. The young
> In one another's arms; birds in the trees,
> — Those dying generations — at their song;
> The salmon falls, the mackerel-crowded seas,
> Fish, flesh or fowl, commend all summer long
> Whatever is begotten, born and dies.
> Caught in that sensual music, all neglect
> Monuments of unageing intellect.
>
> An aged man is but a paltry thing,
> A tattered coat upon a stick, unless
> Soul clap its hands and sing, and louder sing
> For every tatter in its mortal dress,
> Nor is there singing school but studying
> Monuments of its own magnificence;
> And therefore I have sailed the seas and come
> To the holy city of Byzantium.

This verse might be a clarion call to us as we advance in years, a credo for an adult education of the spirit which knows no end. To it we may add the following lines from *T.S. ELIOT*'s 'East Coker':

> Old men ought to be explorers.
> Here and there does not matter
> We must be still and still moving
> Into another intensity
> For a further union, a deeper communion
> Through the dark cold and the empty desolation,
> The wave cry, the wind cry, the vast waters
> Of the petrel and the porpoise. In my end
>   is my beginning.

And this, on the same theme, by *EDMUND WALLER* (1606-1687):

> The seas are quiet when the winds give o'er,
> So calm are we when passions are no more,
> For then we know how vain it was to boast
> Of fleeting things, so certain to be lost.
> Clouds of affection from our younger eyes
> Conceal that emptiness which age descries.
> The soul's dark cottage, battered and decayed,
> Lets in new light through chinks that time has made.
> Stronger by weakness, wiser, men become
> As they draw nearer to their eternal home.
> Leaving the old, both worlds at once they view
> That stand upon the threshold of the new.

So we move to the theme of acceptance of Death, the great transition and release from the 'grave' of the body. The recovery and re-emergence of the spiritual world-view will dispel the spectre of fear of death and bring an inner certainty of the imperishable nature of the soul. In the words of the *BHAGAVAD GITA*:

> Never the spirit was born; the spirit shall cease
> > to be never,
> Never was time it was not; end and beginning
> > are dreams.
> Birthless and deathless and changeless remaineth
> > the spirit forever.
> Death hath not touched it at all, dead though the
> > house of it seems.

A similar truth is expressed by *SIDNEY ROYSE LYSAGHT*:

We have dreamed dreams beyond our comprehending,
   Visions too beautiful to be untrue;
   We have seen mysteries that yield no clue
And sought our goals on ways that have no ending.
We creatures of the earth,
The lowly born, the mortal, the foredoomed
To spend our fleeting moments on the spot
Wherein tomorrow we shall be entombed
And hideously rot —
We have seen loveliness that shall not pass,
We have beheld immortal destinies;
We have seen Heaven and Hell and joined their
   strife;
Ay, we whose flesh shall perish as the grass
Have flung the passion of the heart that dies
Into the hope of everlasting life.

It is worth noting the power of the poem's second line. We can all recognize the mind's capacity to apprehend and seize an idea knowing it to be true by virtue of its very beauty. This may not constitute proof to the cynical intellect, but it may be a stage in the development of latent faculties of perception which may enable us to find a truth in new fields of understanding that cannot be weighed or measured.

The acceptance of the eternal nature of the soul/spirit is fundamental in the change of consciousness now taking place. We are called on to re-think death and abandon the dread, gloom and fear associated with the word. We have no word in our language to express the wondrous process of release into light. Poetry may often help us.

Here is a poem whose author I cannot locate, but which will be moving to those who have experienced bereavement.

> It is eight weeks, beloved, since you died.
> You left the stiffening inert lump of clay
> That was no longer you,
> And cried aloud in ecstasy
> And suddenly I knew
> That all that we believed in,
> Lived for, told the world,
> Had at its smallest count
> Some measure that was true.
>
> It is eight months, beloved, since you died,
> And out of my aloneness I have woven strength
> To build anew;
> For all there was of truth in our relationship
> Had eddied, grown, intensified,

Till with a clarion call it sounds at the far
  reaches of the world —
There is no death, no separation of the ways
If man to love prove true.

It is eight years, beloved, since you died,
And for eternity a part of you
Is in its essence me.
I know you are, and in that certainty
Is woven all the fabric of my life.
Gone is all sense of urgency and haste;
For all time now, our spirits meet in time.
Loving, we are no longer bound by love;
Heart of my heart, we've set each other free.

And this, in a more directly Christian mode, expressing the great hope in a profound but simple way, by *RAYMOND ROSSITER*:

'Christus Consolator'
Beside the dead I knelt in prayer
And felt a presence as I prayed.
Lo, it was Jesus standing there;
He smiled: BE NOT AFRAID.

'Lord, Thou hast conquered death, we know.
Restore again to life', I said,
'This one who died an hour ago.'
He smiled: SHE IS NOT DEAD.

'Asleep, then as Thyself did say.
Yet Thou canst lift the lids that keep
Her prisoned eyes from ours away.'
He smiled: SHE DOTH NOT SLEEP.

'Nay, then, tho' haply she do wake
And look upon some fairer dawn,
Restore her to our hearts that ache.'
He smiled: SHE IS NOT GONE.

'Alas, too well we know our loss,
Nor hope again to feel that breath
Till we ourselves the river cross.'
He smiled: THERE IS NO DEATH.

'Yet our beloved seems so far,
The while we yearn to see them near,
Albeit with Thee we trust they are.'
He smiled: AND I AM HERE.

'Dear Lord, how shall we know that they
Still walk unseen with us and Thee
Nor sleep and wander far away?'
He smiled: ABIDE IN ME.

The great truth that we are here to learn is that the Life Eternal is not a state we go to after death, but is an inner condition of consciousness to be attained now. Of course there is survival, since the soul is imperishable. But mere survival implies mere continuity. And since the next life, beyond the physical world, is a realm of Thought, we find ourselves in the surroundings we can imagine — and therefore strangely like those we have left.

As RADHAKRISHNAN wrote: 'The oldest wisdom in the world tells us we can consciously unite with the divine while in this body; for this man is really born. If he misses his destiny, Nature is not in a hurry; she will catch him up someday, and compel him to fulfil her secret purpose.' This implies we must now work creatively to prepare the condition we are to find in the future. This is finely expressed by *JOHN DONNE*:

> Since I am coming to that Holy Roome
> Where, with Thy Quire of Saints, for evermore
> I shall be made Thy music; as I come
> I tune the instrument here at the door,
> And what I must do then, think here before.

It appears that in our materialistic age, when so many have not won through to belief, the Borderland which all enter after death is crowded with souls unable to make the breakthrough to the so-called Summerland, because they have not been able to free themselves from their negative sceptical thought-forms. Hence the importance for us now to grasp the spiritual world-conception.

RABINDRANATH TAGORE, translating Kabir, impresses this important truth upon us.

> O Friend, hope for Him whilst you live,
> Know while you live, understand while you live:
>   for in life deliverance abides.
> If your bonds be not broken while living
>   What hope of deliverance in death?
> It is but an empty dream, that the soul
> Shall have union with Him because it has
>   passed from the body.
> If He is found now, He is found then.
> If not, we do but go to dwell in the
>   City of Death.
> If you have union now, you shall have it hereafter.

At this point I include five verses from that great poem *FITZGERALD*'s: 'Rubaiyat of Omar Khayyam'.

This is usually treated as a wine-bibber's philosophy — 'Let us eat, drink and be merry for tomorrow we die.' It does, apparently, say that death is extinction — but as we have seen, every symbol is Janus-faced. You are free to read it in the way that gives meaning to your life, negatively or the reverse. Thus the poem really is about Life Eternal, the Wine of Life and consciousness. The Cup is the body, and the wine is the life given us by Him who said, 'I am the true Vine.'

> Think, in this batter'd Caravanserai
> Whose doorways are alternate Night and Day,
> How Sultan after Sultan with his pomp
> Abode his hour or two, and went his way.

The Caravanserai is our Earth life, with the moon-gate of birth and the sun-gate of death — the new dawn.

Listen to this:

> Ah, my Beloved, fill the Cup that clears
> Today of past Regrets and future Fears —
> Tomorrow? — Why, Tomorrow I may be
> Myself with Yesterday's Sev'n Thousand Years.

We must learn to live in the present, not because there is no future but that we have the creation of the future in our own hands, if we can learn to work with our **Higher Self**.

> Ah, fill the Cup, what boots it to repeat
> How Time is slipping underneath our feet:

> Unborn Tomorrow and dead Yesterday,
> Why fret about them if Today be sweet?
>
> One moment in Annihilation's Waste,
> One moment, of the Well of Life to taste —
> The stars are setting and the Caravan
> Starts for the Dawn of Nothing — Oh, make haste!

So easily can the poem look like negation — after death there is nothing. But the Life Eternal belongs to the ethereal realm beyond time, space and form. Thus it is the realm of *No Thing*, a condition of unborn-ness; a freedom from the limitations of form and embodiment. Life on Earth is 'Annihilation's Waste' — this is the 'Well of Life', the heaviest, densest vibration, which we enter for a brief span of existence. As Dawn comes and the stars set, the caravan starts for that Higher Realm — O make haste! Had the negative interpretation been valid, surely Omar would have urged us to miss this Caravan and have another evening of drinking and merry-making. This gives us the clue to the central verse which superficially appears complete negation and, interpreted, is the great affirmation.

> And if the Wine you drink, the Lip you press,
> End in the Nothing all things end in — Yes!
> Then fancy while thou art, thou art but what
> Thou shalt be — Nothing — Thou shalt not be less.

For 'Nothing' read 'No Thing' — a condition of 'pre-thing-ness'.

Note that affirmation of YES in the middle of this strange verse, the assurance that as a soul you will not be less than a free spirit united with your Higher Self. So, while here, imagine you are what you will be — a No Thing. Thus you will prepare for the great transition, with Donne — What you will be then, *think here before*, for Thought is the great reality.

Every verse in this extraordinary poem — Fitzgerald's inspired re-writing of Omar's verses — is a meditation on the Life Eternal and our task of achieving it Now. If you can unravel the poem, it is deeply moving and rewarding. You see that this thinking is not a morbid concern with death and the escape from the body, but a recognition of the infinite beauty and wonder of matter and life, here and now, as the field in which we can achieve the freedom of an expanding of awareness which unites us with the One, the Eternal Life, the Trans-Personal Consciousness.

Among the really great poems in our language is *FRANCIS THOMPSON*'s 'The Hound of Heaven'. The theme is central to all our striving — the ultimate surrender of the soul to God, and His unwavering pursuit of each one of us. In the end we cannot escape this 'tremendous lover'.

Here is the opening verse — space does not allow for more.

I fled Him down the nights and down the days;
  I fled Him down the arches of the years;
I fled Him down the labyrinthine ways
  Of my own mind; and in the mist of tears
I hid from Him, and under running laughter.
      Up vistaed hopes I sped;
      And shot, precipitated,
  Adown Titanic glooms of chasmèd fears,
From those strong feet that followed, followed after.

>   But with unhurrying chase,
>   And unperturbèd pace
>   Deliberate speed, majestic instancy,
>   They beat, and a Voice beat
>   More instant than the Feet —
>   'All things betray thee, who betrayest Me.'

In all our restlessness we begin to glimpse the greater reality:

> Yet ever and anon a trumpet sounds
> From the hid battlements of Eternity;
> Those shaken mists a space unsettle, then
> Round the half-glimpsèd turrets slowly wash again.
>   But not ere him who summoneth
>   I first have seen, enwound
> With glooming robes purpureal, cypress-crowned;
> His name I know, and what his trumpet saith...

The concept of pre-existence, already expressed in the quotations from Wordsworth and Traherne, is in fact more significant than that of mere survival after death, for it raises at once the question of where the spiritual being in us received its education and development.

Here we have to consider the Earth as the great training ground, for the implications are that the soul needs to descend many times into the limitations of the gravity field to learn all the lessons that evolving earth-consciousness can teach. This is expressed remarkably by the American poet *ROBERT FROST* in his poem 'Trial by Existence'.

And from a cliff-top is proclaimed
The gathering of the souls for birth,
The trial by existence named,
The obscuration upon earth...

And the more loitering are turned
   To view once more the sacrifice
Of those who for some good discerned
   Will gladly give up paradise. ...

And none are taken but who will,
   Having first heard the life read out
That opens earthward, good and ill,
   Beyond the shadow of a doubt; ...

Nor is there wanting in the press
   Some spirit to stand simply forth,
Heroic in its nakedness,
   Against the uttermost of earth. ...

But always God speaks at the end:
   'One thought in agony of strife
The bravest would have by for friend,
   The memory that he chose the life;
But the pure fate to which you go
   Admits no memory of choice,
Or the woe were not earthly woe
   To which you gave the assenting voice.'

And so the choice must be again,
   But the last choice is still the same;
And the awe passes wonder then,
   And a hush falls for all acclaim.
And God has taken a flower of gold
   And broken it, and used therefrom

Magic Casements

> The mystic link to bind and hold
>   Spirit to matter till death come.
>
> 'Tis of the essence of life here,
>   Though we choose greatly, still to lack
> The lasting memory at all clear,
>   That life has for us on the rack
> Nothing but what we somehow chose;
>   Thus are we wholly stripped of pride
> In the pain that has but one close,
>   Bearing it crushed and mystified.

The possibility that we were shown our destiny before we descended into incarnation, and actually chose our environment, is well borne out by spiritual research and communication. Rebirth is not put forward as a doctrine to be believed. It is a mystery about which very much needs still to be found out. But note the value of *living as if it were true and you believed it*! If you are prepared to do that, you will have strength and courage to take full responsibility for all you are and for all your circumstances, favourable or difficult. You will never again grumble or try to transfer blame for what you are on to someone or something else! You will become a more positive, tolerant and tolerable member of society.

A great secret lies in this ability to take these great spiritual ideas and live as if you believed them. You have nothing to lose and everything to gain by adopting this plan and you will find it opens the way to exploring into higher truths; and since you are not claiming dogmatic 'belief' there is no need to argue or doubt!

To accept responsibility for our circumstances and to realize the Divine wisdom behind our personal destiny is of first importance. We may take comfort from this poem by *SWAMI VIVEKANANDER*:

THE CUP

This is the cup, the cup assigned to you
    from the beginning.
I know, My child, how much of this dark
    drink is your own brew
Of fault or passion ages long ago
In the deep years of yesterday, I know.

This is your road, a painful road and drear.
I made the stones that never give you rest;
I set your friend in pleasant ways and clear
And he, like you, shall come unto my breast,
But you, My child, must travel here.

This is your task, it has no joy or grace,
But it cannot be wrought by any other hand;
Take it. I do not bid you understand.
I bid you close your eyes and see My face.

We constantly find ourselves returning to the wonder that, within each man, is the centre through which contact and blending with the higher planes of consciousness may be achieved. This is the true communion of man, the coming-of-age of romanticism, the growing up and mature recognition of our real responsibility. For as imperishable spiritual entities, we are truly total cause of our nature and even our circumstances. This is the 'glassy essence' of which Isabella speaks in *SHAKESPEARE*'s 'Measure for Measure':

    Proud man
Dressed in a little brief authority,
Most ignorant of what he's most assured,
His glassy essence, like an angry ape

Plays such fantastic tricks before high heaven
As makes the angels weep.

The same point is reiterated by *BROWNING* in 'Paracelsus':

Truth is within ourselves, it takes no rise
From outward things, whate'er you may believe.
There is an inner centre in us all
Where truth abides in fullness; and around
Wall upon wall the gross flesh hems it in
That perfect clear perception which is Truth.
A baffling and perverting carnal mesh
Binds all and makes all error, but to know
Rather consists in finding out a way
For the imprisoned splendour to escape
Than in achieving entry for a light
Supposed to be without.

Many poets speak in the same vein. Here, for example, is a sonnet by *JOHN MASEFIELD*:

Here in the self is all that man can know
   Of Beauty, all the wonder, all the power
All the unearthly colour, all the glow
   Here in the self that withers like a flower:
Here in the self that fades as hours pass
   And droops and dies and rots and is forgotten
Sooner by ages than the mirroring glass
   In which it sees its glory still unrotten.
Here in the flesh, within the flesh, behind,
   Swift in the blood and throbbing on the bone,
Beauty herself, the universal mind,

Eternal April wandering alone;
The God, the Holy Ghost, the atoning Lord
Here in the flesh, the never-yet explored.

The goal is the flowering of the spirit. It is expressed by a strangely magical modern poem, 'The Tree' by *KARLE WILSON BAKER*:

My life is a tree
Yoke fellow of the earth;
   pledged
By roots too deep for remembrance
To stand hard against the storm
   To fill my place.
(But high in the branches of my green tree
   there is a wild bird singing:
Wind-free are the wings of my bird:
She hath built no mortal nest.)

The same theme is echoed in the following lines by *JUAN RAMON JIMINEZ*:

I have the feeling that my boat has struck,
   down there in the depths
   against some great thing
And nothing happens.
Nothing ... silence ... waves ... nothing.
Or, has everything happened, and are we
   standing quietly now in the new life?

We might also quote another brief poem, 'Indwelling' by *T.E. BROWN*. In their delicate simplicity, these lines express the whole problem of the transformation of the soul in the New Age — the responsibility imposed on each of us to open himself to a higher Self:

> If thou couldst empty all thyself of self
>   Like to a shell dishabited
> Then might He find thee on an ocean shelf
>   And say: This is not dead,
>   And fill thee with Himself instead.
>
> But thou art so replete with very thou
>   And hast such shrewd activity
> That when He comes He'll say: 'It is enow
>   Unto itself. 'Twere better let it be,
>   It is so small and full, and has no need of Me.'

The re-emerging of the ageless wisdom and the quickening of the spirit in our time entails an expansion and acceleration of consciousness, which aspires to apprehend and blend with the whole. At the opening of our epoch, a number of great figures appeared who had achieved a species of cosmic consciousness. These figures included Walt Whitman, AE, W.B. Yeats and Edward Carpenter. All of them were cognisant of the eternal nature of the soul, and also of the fact that it requires many lives to glean the harvest of experience on earth. In the following free verse by *EDWARD CARPENTER*, one can hear the voice of cosmic consciousness, which of course we may identify with the Christ.

> There is no peace except where I am, saith
>   the Lord,
>   I alone remain, I do not change.
>   As space spreads everywhere and all things

> move and change within it,
> But it moves not nor changes,
> So I am the space within the soul, of which
>   the space without
> Is but the similitude or mental image;
> Comest thou to inhabit Me thou hast the
>   entrance to all life —
> Death shall no longer divide thee from those
>   thou lovest.
> I am the sun that shines upon all creatures
>   from within —
> Gazest thou upon Me thou shalt be filled
>   with joy eternal.
> Be not deceived. Soon this outer world shall
>   drop off —
> Thou shalt slough it away as a man sloughs
>   his mortal body.
> Learn even now to spread thy wings in that
>   other world,
> To swim in the ocean, my child, of Me and my
>   love.
> Ah, have I not taught thee by the semblances
>   of this outer
> World, by its alienations and deaths and mortal
>   sufferings — all for this,
>   For Joy, ah joy unutterable.

With such development of the cosmic sense, there will inevitably be a surge of love. We will recognize that the same divinity which burns in ourselves burns in the core of all other living things, and we will salute it in them. The New Age is characterized by the emergence of groups bound by love and a readiness for sacrificial service to the whole. This will entail a deepening and enrichment of personal relationships and of true individuality. For the impulse which fires the New Age is the working of the Avatar of Synthesis. And the promise it holds is echoed by *DAVID GASCOYNE*:

> Not in my life-time, the love I envisage:
> Not in this century it may be. Nevertheless
>   inevitable,
> Having experienced a foretaste of its burning
> And of its consolation, although locked in
>   my aloneness
> Still, although I know it cannot come to be
> Except in reciprocity; I know
> That true love is gratuitous and will race
>   through
> The veins of the reborn world's generations,
>   free
> And sweet, like a new kind of electricity.
>
> The love of heroes and of men like gods
> Has been for long a strange thing on the
>   earth;
> And monstrous to the mediocre. They
> In whom such love is luminous can but
>   transcend
> The squalid inhibitions of those only half
>   alive.
> In blind content they breed who never loved
>   a friend.

In 'A Cosmic Outlook', *FREDERICK MYERS* offers a tremendous vision of the goal and the way:

On! I have guessed the end; the end is fair,
   Not with these weak limbs is thy last race run;
   Not all thy vision sets with this low sun;
Not all thy spirit swoons with this despair.
   Look how thine own soul, throned where all is well
Smiles to regard thy days disconsolate:
   Yea, since herself she wove the wordly spell
Doomed thee for lofty gain to low estate:
   Sown with thy fall a seed of glory fell;
Thy heaven is in thee and thy will thy fate.

Inward! aye deeper far than love or scorn
   Deeper than bloom of virtue, stain of sin,
   Rend thou the veil and pass alone within,
Stand naked there and feel thyself forlorn.
Nay, in what world then, Spirit, wast thou born?
   Or to what World-Soul art thou entered in;
   Feel the self fade, feel the great life begin
With Love re-rising in the cosmic morn.
   The inward ardour yearns to the inmost goal;
The endless goal is one with the endless way;
   From every gulf the tides of Being roll,
From every Zenith burns the indwelling day;
   And life in Life hath drowned thee, soul in Soul
And these are God, and thou thyself art they.

This leads us to the greatest, perhaps, of all themes — the concept of the Christ as a Cosmic Being of Light, Love and Truth, the Essence of all life. We may approach it first through the challenge flung down by *SIDNEY CARTER*, author of 'Lord of the Dance':

        Your holy hearsay
        Is no evidence.

Give me the good news
  In the present tense.

What happened
  Nineteen hundred years ago
May not have happened,
  Who am I to know?

The living truth
  Is what I long to see
I cannot lean upon
  What used to be.

So shut the Bible up
  And show me how
The Christ you talk about
  Is living now.

A reply is offered by the Irish poet, *JOSEPH PLUNKETT*, which strives to express the thought that the Cosmic Christ is present throughout the entire etheric structure of the Earth and, therefore, active in the vital forces which animate all form. Thus to raise our vision to the etheric may be a way to experience an aspect of the Second Coming, which is assuredly the great meaning and mystery of our age.

  I see His blood upon the rose
    And in the stars the glory of His eyes
  His body gleams amid eternal snows
    His tears fall from the skies.

  I see His face in every flower
    The thunder and the singing of the birds

Are but His voice, and carven by His power
   Rocks are His written words.

All pathways by His feet are worn
   His strong heart stirs the ever-beating sea
His crown of thorns is twined with every thorn
   His cross is every tree.

In virtually all his work, GERARD MANLEY HOPKINS, the 'father of modern poetry' was profoundly aware of the Christ principle in living nature. Let us consider an example.

'Hurrahing in Harvest'
Summer ends now; now, barbarous in beauty, the
      stooks arise
   Around; up above, what wind-walks! What
      lovely behaviour
   Of silk sack clouds! has wilder, wilful-wavier
Meal-drift moulded ever and melted across skies?

I walk, I lift up, I lift up heart, eyes,
   Down all that glory in the heavens to glean
      Our Saviour:
   And eyes, heart, what looks, what lips yet
      gave you a
Rapturous love's greeting of realer, of rounder
      replies?

And the azurous hung hills are his world-
      wielding shoulder
   Majestic — as a stallion stalwart, very-violet-
      sweet! —
These things, these things were here and but the
      beholder

Wanting; which two when they once meet,
The heart rears wings bold and bolder
And hurls for him, O half hurls earth for him
off under his feet.

It is worth noting Hopkins' insistence that human initiative is essential if the bridge is to be built. We must lift the heart into the living oneness to find the divine within all matter. Wholeness — the Primal Source — has poured itself into form and therefore self-hood. As divinity and wisdom play into form, an infinite diversity of life emerges, each thing 'selfing', 'going itself'. Hopkins stresses this point in another poem, which for its splendid sounding should rightly be read aloud, with relish:

As kingfishers catch fire, dragonflies draw flame
As tumbled over rim of roundy wells
Stones ring: like each tucked string tells,
    each hung bell's
Bow swung finds tongue to fling out broad his
    name;
Each mortal thing does one thing and the same:
Deals out that spirit indoors each one dwells
Selves — goes itself; MYSELF it speaks and spells
Crying WHAT I DO IS ME: FOR THAT I CAME.

I say more: the just man justices;
Keeps grace: that keeps all his goings graces;
Acts in God's eye what in God's eye he is —
Christ — for Christ plays in ten thousand places
Lovely in limbs, and lovely in eyes not his
To the Father through the features of men's faces.

In short, we must not think of the lower, limited self defined by the personality and the ego. We must think instead of a higher Self which transcends all ephemeral phenomena and issues from — indeed, is one with — the timeless. As Krishna says in the *BHAGAVAD GITA*:

> Wherever there is a withering of the law and
> an uprising of lawlessness on all sides,
> *then* I manifest Myself.
>
> For the salvation of the righteous and the
> destruction of such as do evil, for the firm
> establishing of the Law, I come to birth age
>   after age.

We thus come to the doctrine of the Avatars which runs like a golden thread through all scriptures and history down the ages. When human need is greatest and when the cry of despair goes up, the Saviour manifests. In our age, he is the Avatar of Love, anticipated by the faithful in both hemispheres as the Christ, the Maitreya, the Boddhisatva, the Imam Mahdi, the Messiah. At this point, it is most appropriate to quote 'The Great Invocation', given to the world in 1945, for all who are drawn to the New Age thinking will wish to know and use it.

> From the point of Light within the Mind of God
> Let Light stream forth into the minds of men
> Let Light descend on earth.
>
> From the point of Love within the Heart of God
> Let Love stream forth into the hearts of men
> May Christ return to earth.

> From the centre where the Will of God is known
> Let purpose guide the little wills of men
> The purpose which the Masters know and serve.
>
> From the centre that we call the race of men
> Let the Plan of Light and Love work out
> And may it seal the door where evil dwells.
> LET LIGHT AND LOVE AND POWER
>   RESTORE THE PLAN ON EARTH.

In 'Transfiguration', *EDWIN MUIR* expresses a similar anticipation:

> But He will come again, it's said, though not
> Unwanted and unsummoned; for all things,
> Beasts of the field and woods and rocks and seas
> And all mankind from end to end of the earth
> Will call Him in one voice. In our own time
> Some say, or at a time when time is ripe.
> Then He will come, Christ the uncrucified,
> Christ the discrucified, his death undone,
> His agony unmade, his cross dismantled,
> Glad to be so — and the tormented wood
> Will cure its hurt and grow into a tree
> In a green springing corner of young Eden
> And Judas damned take his long journey backward
> From darkness into light and be a child
> Beside his mother's knee, and the betrayal
> Be quite undone and never more be done.

The coming of the New Age involves a passage through a time of tribulation and this is what we are now experiencing. But 'look up, for your salvation draweth nigh'. It is inevitably an apocalyptic time. We approach the transformation of the age of materialism and egoism. The collapse of outworn forms, the confusion in society — all may be the direct consequence of the pressure of the energies of the living spirit working for the birth of the new society based on harmony and love. And a vision of wholeness nurtures the conviction that the powers of light are indeed pouring themselves into the earth for its redemption, and that, before this century is out, we will indeed have attained a time of transformation. Such transformation will entail not only a physical reclaiming of this polluted planet, but a spiritual one as well — a factor largely ignored in discussions about conservation and ecology. Again, it is *HOPKINS* who suggests what we may hope to witness:

> The world is charged with the grandeur of God.
>   It will flame out, like shining from shook foil;
>   It gathers to a greatness, like the ooze of oil
> Crushed. Why do men then now not reck his rod?
> Generations have trod, have trod, have trod;
>   And all is seared with trade; bleared, smeared
>   with toil;
>   And wears man's smudge and shares man's smell:
>   the soil
> Is bare now, nor can foot feel, being shod.
> And for all this, nature is never spent;
>   There lives the dearest freshness deep down
>   things;
> And though the last lights off the black West went
>   Oh, morning, at the brown brink eastward
>   springs —
> Because the Holy Ghost over the bent
>   World broods with warm breast and with ah!
>   bright wings.

The great change and transformation must begin in each one of us. Since we have been given free-will, we must take responsibility for that point in the Universe which we can really control — our own 'I', which can direct and use body and soul in service of the Whole.

The aspiration to become a clear channel for the 'wind of the spirit' has never been more powerfully expressed than by *D.H. LAWRENCE* in 'The Song of a Man who has Come Through'.

> Not I, not I, but the wind that blows through me!
> A fine wind is blowing the new direction of Time.
> If only I let it bear me, carry me, if only it carry me!
> If only I am sensitive, subtle, Oh delicate,
>   a winged gift!
> If only, most lovely of all, I yield myself and am
>   borrowed
> By the fine, fine wind that takes its course through
>   the chaos of the world
> Like a fine, an exquisite chisel, a wedge-blade
>   inserted;
> If only I am keen and hard like the sheer tip
>   of a wedge
> Driven by invisible blows,
> The rock will split, we shall come at the wonder,
>   we shall find the Hesperides.
> Oh, for the wonder that bubbles into my soul;
> I would be a good fountain, a good well-head,
> Would blur no whisper, spoil no expression.
>
>   What is the knocking?
>   What is the knocking at the door in the night?
>   It is somebody wants to do us harm.

> No, no, it is the three strange angels.
> Admit them, admit them.

Note how he changes his metaphor from the wind to the wedge and how we have to temper ourselves to be the tip of the wedge, so that the invisible worlds may split the cold hard rock of materialistic thinking. Our initiative is vital for the redemptive operation, that we may become effective channels for the creative source and indeed open the door to the 'three strange angels'.

A contemporary poet, *THALIA GAGE*, in her 'Prelude to Pentecost' touches the same note.

> It is not I, Lord, who sing
> But you who sing through me,
> I, but your voice, veiled and broken
> By words,
> But sometimes swinging down the long
>   clear paths
> With your authentic signature of joy.

We enter the Age of Aquarius, an airy sign under which the soul aspires to the living contact with the realm of the Spiritual Sun, which can fire the heart with Love and the mind with Light. *STEPHEN SPENDER* offers us a beautiful vision of the flowering of the spirit:

> I think continually of those who were truly great
> Who from the womb remembered the soul's mysteries
> Down corridors of light where the hours are suns
> Endless and singing. Whose lovely ambition was
> That their lips, still touched with fire

> Should tell of the spirit, clothed head to foot
>   with song.
>   ... What is precious
> Is never to forget ... never to allow
> Gradually the traffic to smother
> With noise and fog the flowering of the spirit.
> Near the snows, near the sun, in the high fields
> See where their names are feted by the waving
>   grass...
> The names of those who in their lives fought
>   for life,
> Who wore in their hearts the fire's centre:
> Born of the sun they travelled a short way
>   towards the sun
> And left the vivid air signed with their honour.

The vision of wholeness implies that the earth is in fact a living sentient creature of which we men are an integral part. To realize our relationship to the wholeness of life we must develop, in Teilhard's phrase, the 'Sense of Earth'. Only in this way may we come to know the Spirit of Earth. We find this principle expressed by *EVELYN NOLT* in 'The Glory Which is Earth':

> Man, tread softly on the Earth
> What looks like dust
> Is also stuff of which galaxies are made.

> The green of Earth's great trees and simple grasses
> Is the same music played in red
> Throughout our trunks and limbs
>
>   The first eye broadcast thought.

Function is the eye of dust.
Fragrance is the flower's eye.
The furred and feathered eye is freedom.
If we cannot see that dust looks back at us
If we will not see thought in the animal
It is because we bind our eyes
To stay Evolution's seeing.

> O Blessed Earth. O patient Earth
> We struggle upward to the Sun
> Forgetting what we as dust knew
> Forgetting what we as flower saw
> Forgetting what we as animal are
> Forgetting humanness is synthesis
> Of dust, flower, animal and something more.

O Earth, living, breathing, thinking Earth
On the day we treasure you
As you have treasured us
Humanness is born.

> And throughout all Light
> A Radiance leaps from star to star
> Singing: A Son is born
> HUMANITY.

Read now an example of the work of that fine New Age poet, the late *GEORGE GRIFFITHS*:

> Darkness would seem to be
> our chosen cloak
> whose very warp and weft's composed
> of suffering
> and death...
> Yet he who knows the ebb and flow of tides

within a tree,
knows too the breath of planets
in their pilgrimage.
Also, in his compass, he would hold in view
the rise and fall
of circumstance
where man, as nexus of two worlds
stands poised at this midbetween
on razor's edge,
gifted beyond angels,
benisoned in light
and cast in the major role...
could he but know it.

We are now entering a time of transfiguration for man. Although the advent of the Aquarian Age is an extended process, this last quarter of our 20th Century will be a time of vital change, with immense hope for man's future. But such change entails a profound responsibility for each of us — a responsibility to think positively, in order that the powers of light may be effectively channelled. In 'A Sleep of Prisoners', *CHRISTOPHER FRY* expresses the urgency incumbent upon us:

> The human heart can go the lengths of God.
> Dark and cold we may be, but this
> Is no winter now. The frozen misery
> Of centuries breaks, cracks, begins to move;
> The thunder is the thunder of the floes,
> The thaw, the flood, the upstart Spring.
> Thank God our Time is now when wrong
> Comes up to face us everywhere,
> Never to leave us till we take

> The longest stride of soul men ever took.
> Affairs are now soul size.
> The enterprise
> Is exploration into God.
> Where are you making for? It takes
> So many thousand years to wake
> But will you wake for pity's sake?

Let us close with a similar admonition from *JAMES ELROY FLECKER:*

> Awake, awake, the world is young
>   For all its weary years of thought.
>   The starkest fights must still be fought,
> The most surprising songs be sung!

And for a final Envoi, this by *F.C. HAPPOLD*, which gives a clarion call for the New Age.

> A wind has blown across the world
>   And tremors shake its frame
> New things are struggling to their birth
>   And naught shall be the same.
> The earth is weary of its past
>   Of folly, hate and fear,
> Behind a dark and stormy sky
>   The dawn of God is near.
>
> A wind is blowing through the Earth
>   A tempest loud and strong.
> The trumpets of the Christ the King
>   Thunder the skies along.
> The summons to a high crusade
>   Calling the brave and true
> To find a New Jerusalem
>   And build the world anew.

Epilogue

The Living Word

The secret of good reciting of poems is simple if we will but note it and follow it. *Speak only the living thought and refuse absolutely to read dead words.* Learn to live solely in the present thought.

If you listen to someone reading or reciting, you will all too often hear that they are being swept on in a desire to read the poem well! The result can be lamentable. Live in the thought. This means that having relished that thought you will pause. The pause between thoughts is the mystery. It is all-important. It may be quite long or it may be very short, but it is absolute. You do this naturally in conversation. Obviously you deliver yourself of a thought and stop — until another thought bubbles up demanding expression. To recite or act is only different in kind. You are speaking not your own thoughts, but someone else's which you must make your own. The moment you are carried away in that terrible drive to 'recite a poem well', nothing will halt you till the last full stop. Listen to a reader. Often a line is followed by an in-sucking of breath. This is absolute proof that the subconscious is *not* living in the present thought, but is obsessed with getting on to the next. To break the habit, the secret is so simple. Having spoken your thought, shut your mouth and allow the lungs gently to refill. Refuse to rush on. Intend only to live in the one thought — then perhaps decide to take yet another thought, and pause again. Try it. This business of shutting your mouth is a way of catching out the unconscious intent. Anxiety will make you breathless at first. Once you have experienced the magic of the 'pregnant pause' you have yourself and your audience in control. Like a good actor, you can do with them what you will. I have *never* heard anyone who pauses too long between thoughts. Broadly speaking, you can afford a surprisingly lengthy pause, for many poems are an essentially meditative experience, and the meaning vibrates and matures and flowers in the silence following the mantric thought. There is at first a natural fear of pausing lest the audience thinks you have broken down. This must be overcome. The tendency for most readers is to take the poem too fast. It is indeed one of the sad illusions that people can grasp and understand a poem at first hearing. This spoils so many recitals, even on B.B.C. A poem is a complex of images stirring the imagination. You must allow time for this process. It is miraculous. I make certain sounds with my voice and in you rises a picture of a spring meadow, a ship, a mountain stream. You cannot stop it, unless you deliberately beat down the rising images with a counter-thought. Sit back and listen, perhaps with closed eyes. A series of linked images forms within you. The inner eye and inner ear are called into action. If, before the picture has fully formed, I throw in another half-baked thought, it will overwhelm the subtle image as it comes to birth and a painful confusion will result. Learn to relish the lovely process to the full and allow long enough for the image to ripen. Then build upon it the next kindred image until a series of pictures are linked.

Here's another secret of good reading aloud. It takes the listener rather longer to grasp the meaning of a thought than it takes you to read the *next* thought. You have the advantage of the written word, and can at a glance get the coming image. Therefore, having spoken the thought, allow your audience time to enjoy and relish it while you shut your mouth and get the next living thought, refusing to speak another line till you have grasped its content and meaning. Of course this means that the first reading must be in somewhat slow motion. It needs to be, since it is an affectation that one hearing alone can unravel the meaning of a complex sonnet. Do not object that the pause is destroying the rhythm. Rhyme and rhythm are magic. They are the inner life and power of the poem. Often their power is more richly experienced when they span the resonant silence. They continue to vibrate. Do you know that the iambic pentameter, the classical Homeric line, really is founded on the rhythmic relationship of heartbeat and breath — four heartbeats to one breath? This is so powerful that it cannot be killed.

Now let us take this delicate and outwardly simple poem by *WALTER de la MARE*.

'*The Song of the Shadows*'
Sweep thy faint strings, musician
   With thy long, lean hand;
      Downward the starry tapers burn,
   Sinks soft the waning sand.
      The old hound whimpers, couched in sleep,
   The embers smoulder low;
      Across the walls the shadows come and go.

Magic Casements

   Sweep softly thy strings, musician;
     The minutes mount to hours.
   Frost on the windless casement weaves
     A labyrinth of flowers.
        Ghosts linger in the darkening air,
        Hearken at the open door,
   Music has called them, dreaming, home once more.

Here is a series of twelve distinct images. Let each one come alight in your imagination and allow the inner picture to form. Then link it with the next one and let the one flow into the other, as on a cinema screen. Obviously, the setting is the hall of a medieval castle with a minstrel harpist. Having voyaged once through the series, go back to the beginning and build them again more strongly, above all linking one picture with the next. Pictures formed in our imagination are alive. Having integrated them, all you need to do is to start at No. 1 and the whole series will flow. If you *really* form living images you could know this poem by heart after three readings. And as you live with the images they become enriched. This poem obviously plays on all the feelings of stilling, quietening, dropping towards sleep. Every image and every sound heighten this meditative experience. At first reading, you'll have formed a general picture of candles and the hour-glass. But how rich in feeling is the linked image:

   'Downward the starry tapers burn
   Sinks soft the waning sand'!

Every word gives a new facet to the whole picture and scene you are imagining.

This is indeed a process of exploring a poem, or rather of exploring your own inner senses and becoming aware of their precious gifts. In de la Mare's poem we are concerned with the inner sight and hearing (the harp music, the whimpering of the dog, the sound of the fire).

When this almost meditative ritual of working into the living ideas in a poem is rightly fulfilled, it is a beautiful soul experience. We all know how painful a bad film may be. By compulsion, images enter through the eye and we cannot protect ourselves from them. In our case of listening to the poem, we alone are monitoring the images and creatively forming the inner pictures. The experience is like a kind of melting of the heart centre, particularly if you are reciting and have got control and stillness in the breathing. (How interesting that we call it 'learning by *heart*'). What I have said holds good, even if the poem is a galloping ballad. The pauses must be absolute, even if only paper-thin. Then every thought is alive.

The poems quoted in this book all lend themselves to the approach here outlined. Explore them in this way. Remember to forbid yourself ever to read dead words. Live in the Living Word, the Living Idea. Know that Ideas are indeed alive, for an idea is a thought-being from the eternal ocean of Thought, which chooses to enter the realm of human thinking through your imagination. Do not hurt these living creatures by your crude reception of their gifts. Welcome them home. They are magic casements...

Such poems as these may indeed be *used* for awakening imagination and intuition. As we said at the beginning of this book, poetry is an aspect of initiation into the higher knowledge, involving those faculties which have so often gone dormant in our over-masculinated intellectual age. But often the magic of poetry is lost through careless and thoughtless recital, which has failed to appreciate what is meant by the Living Idea. In our age of spiritual awakening, the Ageless Wisdom appears to be breaking through into our consciousness. It is as if there were an ocean of living wisdom on the ethereal plane beyond time and form. Our lifted thinking and expanded consciousness can begin to tap this reservoir, and channel the archetypal ideas. And they are the stuff of great poetry.

One approach I have touched on clearly differs from the usual academic study. We are avowedly founding our approach on the holistic world-view, which accepts the spiritual nature of man and the universe. When, with this world-picture in mind, we approach the great works of art and literature, they often begin to speak in a new way. We may sense the need for re-interpretation in the light of the spiritual world-view. This is something more than the 'onlooker' approach of academic criticism. It implies a blending with the being and beings within the forms. The symbols in myth and legend, poetry and drama, begin to speak to us, enhancing the meaning of life. Surely in our benighted world this gift is of unparalleled importance. Are we not being invited to a re-exploring of the arts seen as a vehicle for the living spirit, for this surely is what lies behind the creation of the master works? If we can but learn how to read these works aright, shall we not be resonating with the thinking of the initiate-souls who created them? The arts are truly the gateway to spiritual knowledge and should be approached as such. The

Magic Casements

present volume is an extremely modest attempt at such an approach. It could be followed by others. The rich heritage of English poetry holds so many treasures which we can use for the awakening of consciousness.